Contents

YO-ELK-627

Contents
Three Cheers for August 1–2, SV 9835-3

Meets **Accreditation Standard** for Child-created Bulletin Boards

Three Cheers for August 1–2, SV 9835-3

Introduction

This series of monthly activity books is designed to give first and second grade teachers a collection of hands-on activities and ideas for each month of the year. The activities are standards-based and reflect the philosophy that children have different styles of learning. The teacher can use these ideas to enhance the development of the core subjects of language, math, social studies, and science, as well as the social/emotional and physical growth of children. Moreover, the opportunity to promote reading skills is present throughout the series and should be incorporated whenever possible.

Organization and Features

Each book consists of seven units:

Unit 1 provides reproducible pages and information for the month in general.
- a newsletter outline to promote parent communication
- a blank thematic border page
- a list of special days in the month
- calendar ideas to promote special holidays
- a blank calendar grid that can also be used as an incentive chart

Units 2–6 include an array of activities for five **theme** topics. Each unit includes
- teacher information on the theme
- arts and crafts ideas
- a food activity
- poetry, language skills (songs, poems, raps, and chants), and books
- bulletin board ideas
- center activities correlated to specific learning standards (Language arts, math, science, social studies, and writing are included in each theme.)

Implement the activities in a way that best meets the needs of individual children.

Unit 7 focuses on a well-known **children's author**. The unit includes
- a biography of the author
- activities based on a literature selection
- a list of books by the author
- reproducible bookmarks

In addition, each book contains
- reproducible **icons** suitable to use as labels for centers in the classroom. The icons coordinate with the centers in the book. They may also be used with a work assignment chart to aid in assigning children to centers.
- reproducible **student awards**
- **calendar day pattern** with suggested activities

Research Base

Howard Gardner's theory of multiple intelligences, or learning styles, validates teaching thematically and using a variety of approaches to help children learn. Providing a variety of experiences will assure that each child has an opportunity to learn in a comfortable way.

Following are the learning styles identified by Howard Gardner.
- **Verbal/Linguistic** learners need opportunities to read, listen, write, learn new words, and tell stories.
- **Bodily/Kinesthetic** learners learn best through physical activities.
- **Musical** learners enjoy music activities.
- **Logical/Mathematical** learners need opportunities to problem solve, count, measure, and do patterning activities.
- **Visual/Spatial** learners need opportunities to paint, draw, sculpt, and create artworks.
- **Interpersonal** learners benefit from group discussions and group projects.
- **Intrapersonal** learners learn best in solitary activities, such as reading, writing in journals, and reflecting on information.
- **Naturalist** learners need opportunities to observe weather and nature and to take care of animals and plants.
- **Existential** learners can be fostered in the early years by asking children to think and respond, by discussions, and by writing.

Gardner, H. (1994). *Frames of mind.* New York: Basic Books.

August News

Teacher:_____ Date:_____

Headline News

Coming Up

Happy Birthday to

Special Thanks to

Help Wanted

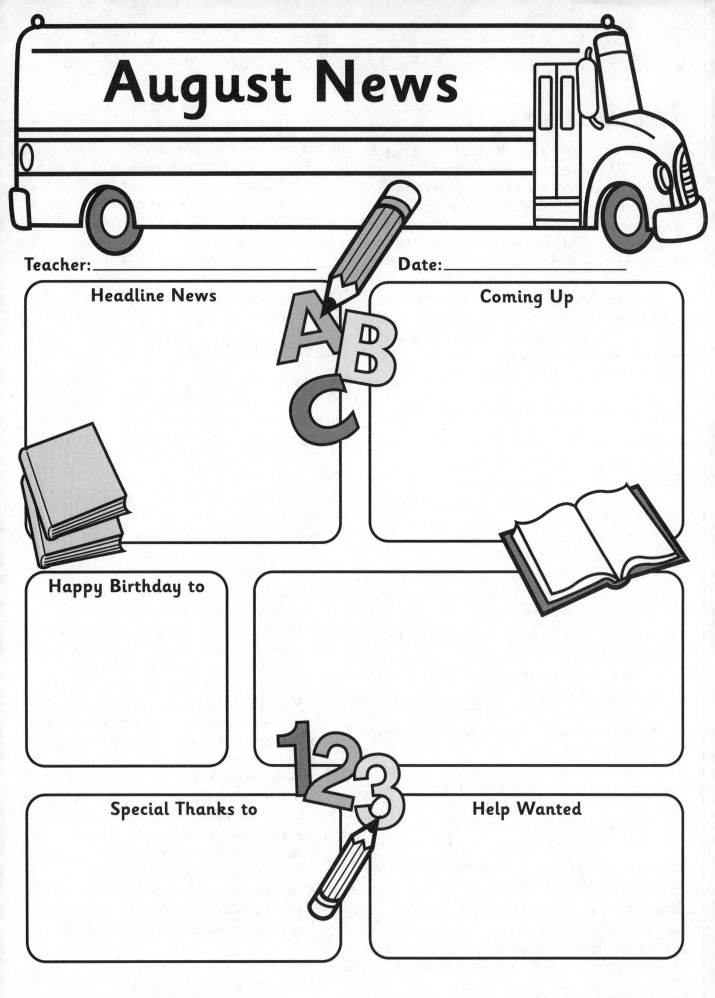

Three Cheers for August 1–2, SV 9835-3

August

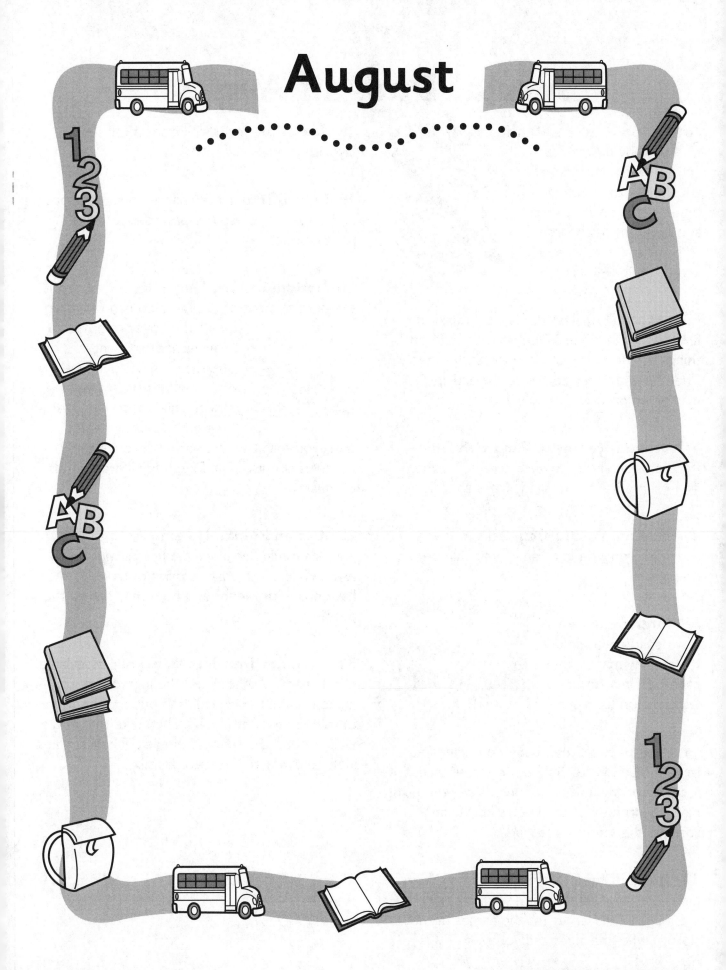

Three Cheers for August 1–2, SV 9835-3

Special Days in August

Artist Appreciation Month Display the art of well-known American artists. Lead a discussion about how the work of one artist is different from another's. Invite children to paint at the easel and create their own art.

Friendship Day This day is celebrated the first Sunday in August. Discuss with children things that friends would do for each other. Then have children complete the activity master on page 9.

2 National Ice-Cream Sandwich Day Read a book about how ice cream is made. Then serve ice-cream sandwiches to children.

3 American Family Day Celebrate with activities from the In a Family unit that begins on page 41.

3 Watermelon Day Have children complete the activity master on page 10. Then serve watermelon for a snack.

11 Play in the Sand Day Pour sand in a large tub and invite children to experience it. If focusing on a particular phonics skill, you might have children write the letters in glue and sprinkle the sand on the glue.

12 Middle Child Day Have children draw a picture of their family. Invite volunteers who are middle children to tell the names of their siblings who are older and younger.

16 Joke Day Invite children to tell their favorite jokes.

19 Potato Day Have children peel potatoes and grate them. Use the potatoes to make potato soup.

20 National Radio Day Place books about the development of the radio and an old radio

with the cover removed in the technology center. (Radios can be found cheaply in thrift stores.) Invite children to explore the parts. During center time, you might wish to move through the channels and listen and identify different kinds of music.

25 Kiss and Make Up Day Read aloud *The Berenstain Bears and the Trouble with Friends.* Invite children to share stories of troubles they have had with friends and how they solved the problem.

31 National Trail Mix Day Bring resealable plastic bags to school and the ingredients to make trail mix. Have children put a tablespoon of each ingredient in bags. Then take them on a walk around the school complex. Take a break along the way to eat the trail mix.

August

Sunday	Monday	Tuesday	Wednesday	Thursday	Friday	Saturday

Using the Calendar for Basic Introduction in the Classroom

The children you teach may enjoy using the calendar-related games and activities on this page to practice other skills.

Word Problems   During daily calendar time, practice problem solving by asking children to use the calendar to answer a question. For example: It rained all week except on Monday, Wednesday, and Thursday. On which days did it rain? You may wish to relate the questions to holidays or units of study.

Graphing   Make a line graph to hang on the wall. Write the numbers 1–6 on the vertical axis and the twelve months of the year on the horizontal axis. Find out how many children have a birthday in each month and record on the graph. Connect the points to finish the line graph. You may wish to have the children copy the data and make individual line graphs.

Patterning   Give children a calendar page for any month that you choose. Decide on a specific color pattern, such as red, yellow, and green. Have children color three days in the middle of the calendar red, yellow, and green. Then, have them color all of the remaining days using the same pattern. They will be extending patterns forward and backward.

Math Facts   Have children play a calendar toss game. Make a large calendar page on a plastic tablecloth and lay it on the floor. Select a number that the children need to practice with addition, subtraction, multiplication, or division facts (for example, subtracting the number 9). Give players one beanbag each and have children take turns tossing the beanbag on the calendar. Each player will subtract the number 9 from the number that the beanbag lands on. You may wish to have them write the equation.

Distances on a Number Grid   Give children a calendar page of your choice. Have them find how many spaces they move from one number to another number Example: How many spaces do you move to go from 17 to 23?

Coin Values   Assign a coin value to consonant letters and a coin value to vowel letters. Using the assigned values, have children total the value of each of the days of the week or the months of the year. Challenge them to find out which is worth more or less or compare one to another. You may wish to name a specific amount at the beginning of the activity and have children find out which day of the week or month is equal to that amount.

Special Days   Calendars are full of celebrations of all types. These special days are fun and exciting for children. However, children may not know why various holidays are celebrated. You may wish to use the activity masters on pages 9 and 10 to expand their knowledge of favorite holidays and special days. The information for these special days is included below.

August is the one month of the year that does not have any national holidays. The activity masters for this month highlight the more light-hearted days of Friendship Day and Watermelon Day.

- **National Friendship Day** is the first Sunday in August. In 1935, the United States Congress proclaimed a special day to honor friends.
- **Watermelon Day** is August 3. It is a day honoring a favorite summer fruit. Using the watermelon slice on page 10 as a model, draw a large watermelon on craft paper. Give each seed a value from 1 to 5. Then invite children to play a game.

Name _____ Date _____

National Friendship Day

Directions: Choose the name of one of your friends. Write the name in the boxes below with only one letter in each box. Keep writing the name over and over until you fill all of the boxes. Look to see if there is a pattern.

Watermelon Day

Directions: Play a game. Toss a beanbag on the seeds five times.
Write each number that your beanbag lands on this paper. Add
the numbers together. Compare the total with a partner.

Fact-oring in School

 In Colonial times, boys and girls did not go to school together. A schoolmaster, usually a minister, taught the boys. They learned the subjects of reading, calligraphy (writing), math, and language (usually French).

 Colonial girls learned calligraphy, sewing, dance, and etiquette (social manners).

 Colonial children did not have books. They were very expensive. Children learned to read and write from a hornbook. A hornbook was a small, wooden paddle with one sheet of paper glued to the front. The alphabet, some letter pairs, and a Bible verse were often included on the hornbook.

 To protect the expensive paper on the hornbook, parents or teachers covered it with a very thin layer of a cow's horn. The horn was cut so thin that the print on the paper showed through.

 A battledore replaced the hornbook when paper became less expensive. It was an early kind of reading book. It was a rectangle paper folded into thirds. It included the alphabet in capital and small letters. Some battledores had word lists and a short story or fable.

 Pioneer children attended school from October to May. They went to school six days a week. This schedule made it possible for them to be home during the planting and harvest seasons.

 Pioneer children only went to school through the eighth grade, and all grades were taught in one room. However, most children only attended school to the age of eight or nine because they were needed to work on the farm.

 Most of the time, pioneer children had to memorize their lessons. They wrote on slate, the early form of blackboards.

11

Unit 2, Time for School: Teacher Information
Three Cheers for August 1–2, SV 9835-3

A Book from the Past

Materials

- pattern on page 20
- recycled file folders
- white construction paper
- markers
- scissors
- glue

Directions

Teacher Preparation: Trace several hornbook patterns to use as templates on file folders and cut them out. Cut apart the remaining file folders so they are the size of a hornbook. Each child will need one folder. Cut white construction paper into 4" x 5" rectangles. Discuss with children the history of the hornbook on page 11.

1. Trace a hornbook on a folder. Cut out the hornbook.
2. Get a white paper rectangle.
3. Write the capital letters across the top of the rectangle.
4. Write the lowercase letters across the bottom of the rectangle.
5. Glue the rectangle on the hornbook.

Hang Me Up

Materials

- patterns on page 21
- markers or crayons
- scissors
- construction paper
- clear contact paper (or laminating supplies)
- glue

Directions

Teacher Preparation: Duplicate a hanger for each child. Cut two pieces of contact paper that are slightly larger than the hanger for each child.

Note: You may wish to have children make several hangers to decorate cubbies, desks, chairs, and shelves. The hangers can also be used in centers to identify which children may be in each area.

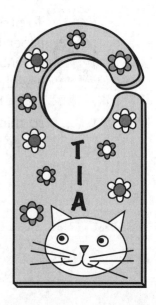

1. Cut out a hanger.
2. Write your name on one side of the hanger.
3. Think of things that you like or enjoy doing. Draw pictures of these things on both sides of the hanger.
4. Cover the hanger with clear contact paper. Cut around the edges of the hanger and inside the circle to cut off the extra parts.

Hornbook Sandwich

You will need

- wheat bread
- pretzel sticks
- spreadable cream cheese
- raisins
- craft sticks
- paper towels

Directions

1. Put a piece of bread on a paper towel.
2. Spread cream cheese on the bread.
3. Use raisins to write some alphabet letters.
4. Push a pretzel stick into the side of a piece of bread.

Note: Be aware of children who may have food allergies.

Three Cheers for August 1–2, SV 9835-3

Back to School Rap

Time to grab my pencil,

And my new backpack.

Make a peanut butter sandwich,

And put it in a sack.

I'm gonna' board that bus,

So I can get to school.

I wanna' read and write,

And learn the Golden Rule!

(chorus)

Back to school—

Yeah, it's time for school.

Back to school—

Yeah, school is cool!

I'm gonna' meet my teacher,

And lots of new friends.

Gonna' have such fun,

That I hope it doesn't end.

But when it's time for work,

I'll have to quiet down.

I'll listen, and I'll look,

And I won't make a sound!

(chorus)

Books to Learn About Learning

Back to School for Rotten Ralph
by Jack Gantos (HarperCollins)

First Day Jitters
by Julie Danneberg (Charlesbridge Publishing)

If You Take a Mouse to School
by Laura Joffe Numeroff (HarperCollins)

My First Day of School
by P.K. Hallinan (Ideas Publications)

My School, Your School
(Raintree/Steck-Vaughn)

My Teacher's My Friend
by P.K. Hallinan (Ideas Publications)

My Teacher Sleeps in School
by Leatie Weiss (Puffin)

Schools Around the World
by Donald Mitchell (Steck-Vaughn)

Teacher from the Black Lagoon
by Mike Thaler (Scholastic)

Walter the Lazy Mouse
by Marjorie Flack (Doubleday & Company)

Materials

- pattern on page 22
- light green construction paper
- light blue and brown craft paper
- green border
- children's pictures
- crayons or markers
- scissors
- glue
- stapler

Directions

Teacher Preparation: Duplicate the lettuce pattern on the green construction paper for each child. Cover the top quarter of the board with the blue craft paper. Cover the bottom of the board with the brown craft paper. Use a green corrugated border to simulate garden rows as well as a decorative border. Add the caption across the blue paper. You may wish to include a sign with "[teacher's name]'s Garden."

1. Cut out a head of lettuce.

2. Draw a picture on the lettuce that shows something you do well.

3. Glue a copy of your picture on the lettuce.

Allow children time to explain their picture to the class. Help them staple their pictures in rows of the garden.

Schooling Centers

Language Center

Language Arts Standard
Knows the order of the alphabet

We're Tired

Materials

- patterns on page 23
- file folders
- scissors
- white construction paper
- markers
- glue

Teacher Preparation: Duplicate two copies of the bus and tire patterns page on white construction paper. Color the buses and tires and cut them out. Decide if you will use capital or lowercase letters or a combination of both. (You may want to make multiple folders to address several skills.) On the buses, write letters of the alphabet that have letters that come before and after them. (Do not use *A* or *Z*.) Glue the six buses to the inside of a file folder. On the tires, write the letters that are sequentially to the left and right of the letters on the bus.

Invite children to place the tires on each bus in the correct alphabetical order.

Note: For more of a challenge, write phonograms on the buses. Write initial letters that complete the words on the tires for children to match.

Social Studies Center

Social Studies Standard
Creates and uses simple maps to identify the location of places in the classroom, school, community, and beyond

Map It!

Materials

- sentence strips
- marker
- tape

Teacher Preparation: Make labels on sentence strips for important pieces of furniture and areas in the classroom. Tape the labels on the furniture or in the area. Then make a simple map of the classroom. Add arrows and writing lines to the areas on the map that match the labels. Duplicate a map for each child.

Have partners use the map to walk around the room and identify the parts shown on the map. Tell them to write the labeled words on their maps.

Schooling Centers

Science Center

Science Standard
Sorts organisms and objects according to their parts and characteristics

Pack the Backpack

Materials

- activity master on page 24
- crayons

Teacher Preparation: Duplicate the activity master for each child.

Have children color the school supplies they can put into a backpack.

Math Center

Math Standard
Counts and recognizes numbers 99

Count Out

Materials

- pattern on page 20
- index cards
- counting cubes
- glue
- brown and white construction paper
- marker
- scissors

Teacher Preparation: Duplicate the hornbook pattern on brown construction paper. Cut out a 4" x 5" white rectangle for each hornbook. Glue the rectangle on the hornbook to make workmats. Write numbers on index cards that you wish children to practice and understand.

Have children stack the cards and lay the stack facedown on a table. Have children take turns choosing a card and modeling the number with cubes on a hornbook workmat.

Note: For more of a challenge, have partners compare their numbers to identify whose numbers are larger or smaller.

Schooling Centers

Writing Center

Language Arts Standard
Understands that written words are separated by spaces

School Is Cool

Materials

- paper
- crayons

Review the "Back to School Rap" on page 14. Invite children to draw a picture of why they think school is cool. Have them write a sentence or paragraph to go along with their picture. Remind them to use a finger space to separate the words in a sentence.

Technology Center

Technology Standard
Uses technology terminology appropriate to the task

Meet the Computer

Materials

- activity master on page 25
- sentence strips
- crayons or markers
- tape
- keyboard
- computer
- mouse

Teacher Preparation: Duplicate the activity master for each child. Use sentence strips to make labels for the monitor, keyboard, and mouse. Tape the labels on the corresponding parts of the computer.

Review the parts of a computer with children. Then have them label the parts of the computer. Ask them to color the keys they would use to type their first names.

Schooling Centers

Game Center

Lunchbox Toss

Materials

- a variety of lunchboxes
- masking tape
- 3 beanbags
- scrap paper
- index cards
- markers

Teacher Preparation: Write point values from 1 to 3 on index cards. Make a card for each lunchbox. Make a tape line on the floor to designate where players will stand. Place the lunchboxes at different distances from the line. Tape a point value card to the outside of each box, giving lunchboxes with small openings or those placed at a great distance from the tape line high values.

Invite children to take turns tossing the beanbags at the lunchboxes and recording their scores for each beanbag that lands inside a lunchbox. The first to reach 10 points is the winner.

Literacy Center

Today's Battledore

Materials

- 11" x 17" light-colored construction paper
- chart
- crayons
- marker

Teacher Preparation: Make a copy of a battledore for children to follow. (See the teacher information on page 11.) Include the capital and lowercase alphabet. Draw pictures and write a familiar story or nursery rhyme. On a chart, write important sight words or words that the children need to know in spelling or another subject to make the word list.

Discuss with children the history of the battledore. Then invite children to make a battledore. Have them include capital and lowercase letters, a word list, and a story or nursery rhyme. They can decorate the other panels with their own pictures and stories.

Hornbook Pattern

Use with "A Book from the Past" on page 12, "Count Out" on page 17, and "Facing Our Feelings" on page 30.

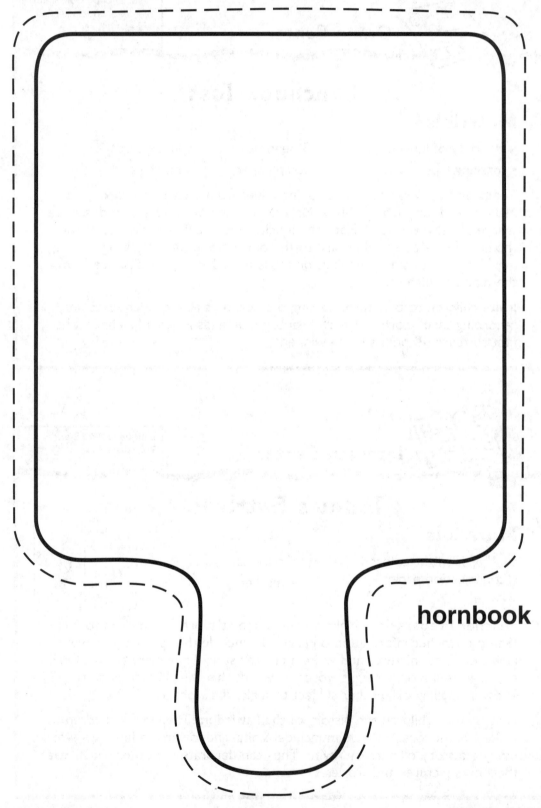

hornbook

Hanger Patterns

Use with "Hang Me Up" on page 12.

hangers

Lettuce Pattern

Use with " 'Lettuce' Meet Our Friends" on page 15.

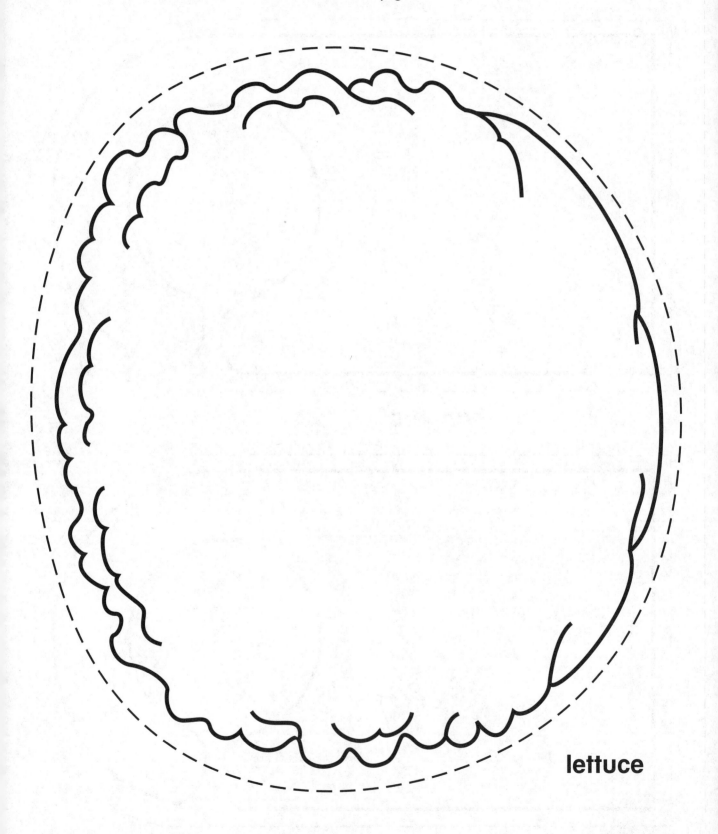

lettuce

Three Cheers for August 1–2, SV 9835-3

Bus and Tires Patterns

Use with "We're Tired" on page 16.

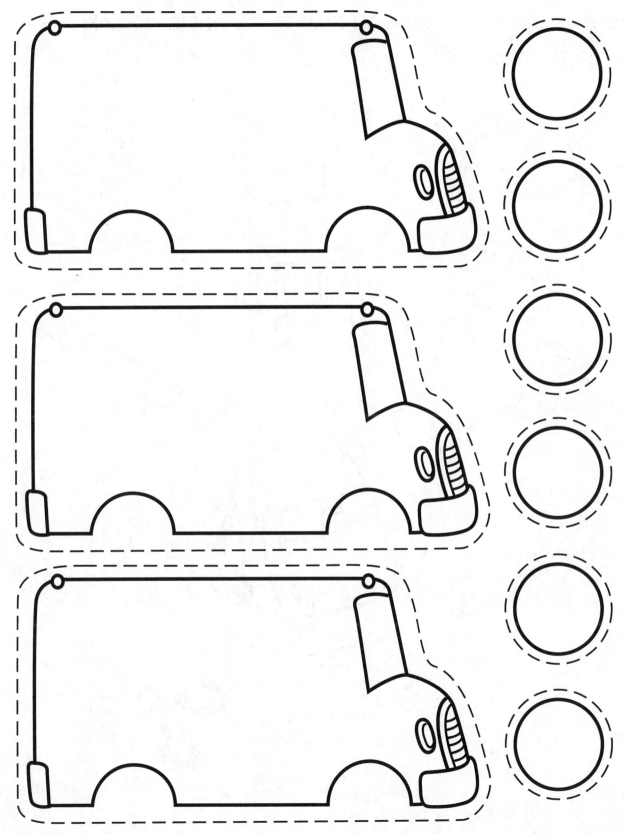

Three Cheers for August 1–2, SV 9835-3

Name _____ Date _____

Pack Up for School

Directions: What can you take to school in a backpack?
Color the pictures.

Use with "Pack the Backpack" on page 17.

Unit 2, Time for School: Activity Master
Three Cheers for August 1–2, SV 9835-3

Name _____   **Date** _____

Computer

Directions: Label the parts of the computer. Color the keys you would use to type your first name.

Use with "Meet the Computer" on page 18 and "I Live Here" on page 63.

Unit 2, Time for School: Activity Master and Pattern
Three Cheers for August 1–2, SV 9835-3

Fact Feelings

 People use 26 muscles to smile and 62 muscles to frown.

Smiling actually promotes the nervous system to produce a chemical that gives a pleasant feeling to the whole body. Likewise, a frown often causes increased blood flow to the feet and hands, a sign of anger.

The most famous smile is a painting of a Florence lady—Lisa. Leonardo da Vinci painted *Mona Lisa* between 1503 and 1506. It is an oil painting that is about 30 x 21 inches.

Stress can affect the emotional state of a person and lead to physical health problems as well.

Colors often have emotional meanings. Blue means sad, green means jealous, and red means angry.

The feelings you have about yourself is called self-esteem.

When people experience strong emotions, it is because chemicals, called endorphins, are released into their brains. Endorphins make people feel happy, sad, angry, etc.

Anger can make a person feel hot or cold. The heartbeat quickens and breathing may become short and rapid. The muscles may feel tight and cause the person to feel shaky or sick to his or her stomach.

An angry response causes chemical changes in the body that result in extra strength and alertness. It is the body's way to help protect the person from danger.

Babies are not born with the ability to control their feelings. They have to learn what to do with the emotions. Learning to control different feelings is called self-control. People work to learn self-control their whole lives.

Sometimes people experience several different feelings at once. These are called mixed feelings.

I Am Feeling

Materials

- patterns on pages 35 and 36
- paper plates
- brads
- yarn
- markers
- scissors
- glue
- hole punch

Directions

Teacher Preparation: Duplicate one copy of each page of the patterns for each child.

1. Divide a paper plate into eight equal parts.

2. Color and cut out the eight faces.

3. Glue one face in each part of the paper plate.

4. Cut out a spinner from another paper plate.

5. Use a brad to attach the spinner to the center of the plate.

6. Punch two holes near the top of the plate.

7. Cut a piece of yarn.

8. Tie each end of the yarn around a hole.

Note: Invite children to hang the plates on their chairs and move the arrow to the feeling they are experiencing at different times of the day.

Name That Feeling

Materials

- recycled magazines
- construction paper
- markers
- glue
- scissors
- chart paper

Directions

Teacher Preparation: Brainstorm with children a list of different kinds of feelings and write their responses on chart paper. Display the chart.

1. Cut out pictures from magazines of at least eight different feelings.

2. Number each picture.

3. On construction paper, write the numbers and the names of the matching feelings beside them.

4. Turn the paper over and glue the pictures on the paper in any order to form a collage. Be careful not to cover up a number.

5. When the collages are dry, trade papers with a partner. Name the feelings.

Spotty-Dotty Faces

You will need

- peanut butter
- powdered milk
- honey
- raisins
- plastic cups
- craft sticks
- cupcake liners
- tablespoons
- teaspoons

Directions

1. Put 1 tablespoon of peanut butter in a cup.
2. Add 2 tablespoons of powdered milk.
3. Add 1 teaspoon of honey.
4. Mix with a craft stick.
5. Roll the dough into 2 balls.
6. Flatten both balls and put each in a cupcake liner.
7. Use the raisins to make faces illustrating two different feelings.
8. Tell a partner the feelings on the faces before eating them.

Note: Be aware of children who may have food allergies.

Mother Goose Land

I had a dream about Mother Goose,

And all the characters were running loose.

Here are some of the things that I was seeing,

And some of the feelings they were feeling.

Little Miss Muffet was very afraid.

But Mary was proud of her pretty maids.

The little dog laughing was certainly glad.

But a fish that bit me must have been mad.

Little Boy Blue was feeling sleepy.

Those three little kittens were sad and weepy.

Bo Peep was worried about her little lost sheep.

Jack was so nimble, he was surprised by his leap.

When I awoke, it was nearly dawn.

I was lonely—Mother Goose land was gone.

Note: Repeat the poem several times. As children become familiar with the feelings, pause and allow them to supply the feeling words. Challenge children to name and recite the nursery rhymes that the emotions reference.

Feeling Good About These Books . . .

Feelings
by Aliki (Dimensions)

The Feelings Book
by Todd Parr (Megan Tingley)

The Feelings Box
by Ronald M. Gold (Aegina Press)

I Feel Orange Today
by Patricia Goodwin and Kitty Macaulay
(Annick Press)

Today I Feel Silly: And Other Moods That Make My Day
by Jamie Lee Curtis (Joanna Cotler)

The Way I Feel
by Janet Cain (Parenting Press)

When Sophie Gets Angry—Really, Really Angry
by Molly Bang (Scholastic)

Facing Our Feelings

Materials

- patterns on pages 20, 35, and 36
- construction paper in a variety of colors
- foil
- white craft paper
- border
- markers
- stapler
- scissors
- tape

Directions

Teacher Preparation: To make the hand-held mirrors, duplicate the hornbook pattern from page 20 on different colors of paper. Enlarge and duplicate the face patterns from pages 35 and 36 on white paper. Color and cut out the faces. Cover the bulletin board with white paper, add a border, and staple the faces in a random arrangement. Cut foil into 4" x 5" rectangles.

1. Choose your favorite color of construction paper.

2. Cut out the mirror.

3. Tape a foil rectangle in the center of the mirror.

Discuss how the face and body show different emotions. Then say the names of different emotions and have children show the feelings with their faces and bodies. Lead them in a discussion of how to identify their emotions and the proper outlets to express them. Finally, help children staple their mirrors on the bulletin board.

Note: You might use the phrase "facing your feelings" as a clue that children need to stop and consider their emotions and actions.

Feeling Good Centers

Language Center

Language Arts Standard
Applies letter-sound correspondences

Happy About Sounds

Materials

- activity master on page 37
- crayons

Teacher Preparation: Duplicate the activity master for each child.

Review each picture name. Then have children write the missing letter. Invite them to color the things on the page that make them happy.

Math Center

Math Standard
Recognizes and creates shapes that have symmetry

Half a Face

Materials

- activity master on page 38

Teacher Preparation: Duplicate the activity master for each child.

Ask children to draw the other half of the face so it looks like the part that they see. Then have them circle the name of the feeling that the face shows.

Feeling Good Centers

Science Center

Science Standard
Explains a problem and identifies a solution

Picture Problems

Materials

- recycled magazines
- construction paper
- glue
- scissors
- markers or crayons

Teacher Preparation: Cut out from magazines multiple pictures of people in situations who are showing strong, negative emotions, such as a woman looking at dirty footprints on carpet. Glue the pictures on construction paper.

Invite partners to choose a picture, identify the emotions and the problem, and brainstorm solutions. Have them draw a picture of one of their solutions.

Social Studies Center

Social Studies Standard
Identifies traditions in their families

Favorite Family Tradition

Materials

- paper
- markers or crayons

Invite children to discuss their favorite family holidays. Encourage children who experience interesting cultural differences to share as much information as they can. Then have children draw a picture of their favorite family holiday. Ask them to dictate or write a sentence to go along with their picture.

Feeling Good Centers

Writing Center

Language Arts Standard
Uses basic capitalization
and punctuation

Pictures Worth 1,000 Words

Materials

- favorite picture books
- chart paper
- self-stick notes
- marker

Tell children that words people say are put in quotation marks when they are printed. Then demonstrate several examples on chart paper. Invite children to select a favorite book. Have them skim the illustrations to find a picture with two or more characters. Challenge children to write sentences that the characters might be saying on the self-stick notes. Tell them to place the notes above the heads of the characters.

Technology Center

Technology Standard
Uses a variety of input
devices such as mouse,
keyboard, and disk drive

Feeling a Font Change

Materials

- chart listing different emotions completed in "Name That Feeling" on page 27
- computer
- keyboard
- mouse
- printer

Display and discuss the chart. Invite children to type the word that describes the feeling they are presently experiencing. Have them copy and paste or type the word several times. Invite them to explore changing the word into several different fonts. Help them print the page. Ask them to circle the font they like best.

Feeling Good Centers

Literacy Center

Language Arts Standard
Uses synonyms, antonyms, and homonyms

Feeling Opposite

Materials

• activity master on page 39

Teacher Preparation: Duplicate the activity master for each child.

Help children read the words in the box and the clues. Then have them complete the puzzle. For children needing additional support, pair them with children who are familiar with crossword puzzles.

Communication Center

Social Studies Standard
Expresses ideas orally based on knowledge and experiences

Rolling with the Feeling

Materials

• pattern on page 40
• crayons
• clear tape

• white construction paper
• scissors
• glue

Teacher Preparation: Duplicate the cube pattern on white paper. Draw and color a face showing a different feeling on each of the squares. Cut out the cube, fold it on the lines, and glue it as indicated. Tape the edges to make the cube stronger.

Invite children to take turns rolling the cube. Have them name the feeling and identify a situation when that feeling might be experienced.

Faces of Feelings Patterns

Use with "I Am Feeling" on page 27 and "Facing Our Feelings" on page 30.

happy

angry

afraid

silly

Faces of Feelings Patterns

Use with "I Am Feeling" on page 27 and "Facing Our Feelings" on page 30.

sad

surprise

worry

loving

Unit 3, Face the Feelings: Patterns

Three Cheers for August 1–2, SV 9835-3

Name _____ Date _____

Happiness Is . . .

Directions: Say each picture name. What sound is missing? Write the letter. Then color the pictures of the things that make you happy.

1.  _____ og	2.  _____ ing	3.  _____ ig
4.  _____ est	5.  _____ at	6.  _____ an
7.  _____ ell	8. 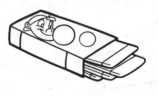 _____ um	9.  _____ ask

Use with "Happy About Sounds" on page 31.

Unit 3, Face the Feelings: Activity Master
Three Cheers for August 1–2, SV 9835-3

Make a Face

Directions: Draw the other part of the face. Make it look the same.

What feeling do you see? Circle the word.

happy   **surprised**   **angry**

Use with "Half a Face" on page 31.

Name _____ Date _____

Crossword Opposites

Directions: Read each clue. Write a word from the box that means the opposite. Then write the word in the puzzle. Circle words that are about feelings.

| hot | girl | near | under | laugh | found |

Across

4. far _____

5. cry _____

Down

1. boy _____

2. over _____

3. lost _____

6. cold _____

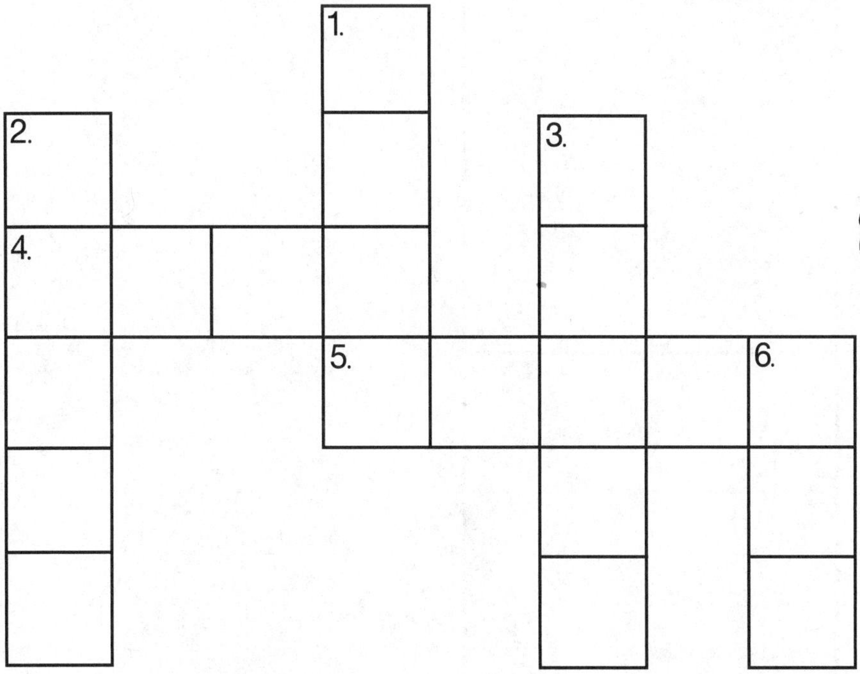

Use with "Feeling Opposite" on page 34.

Unit 3, Face the Feelings: Activity Master
Three Cheers for August 1–2, SV 9835-3

Feelings Cube Pattern

Use with "Rolling with the Feeling" on page 34.

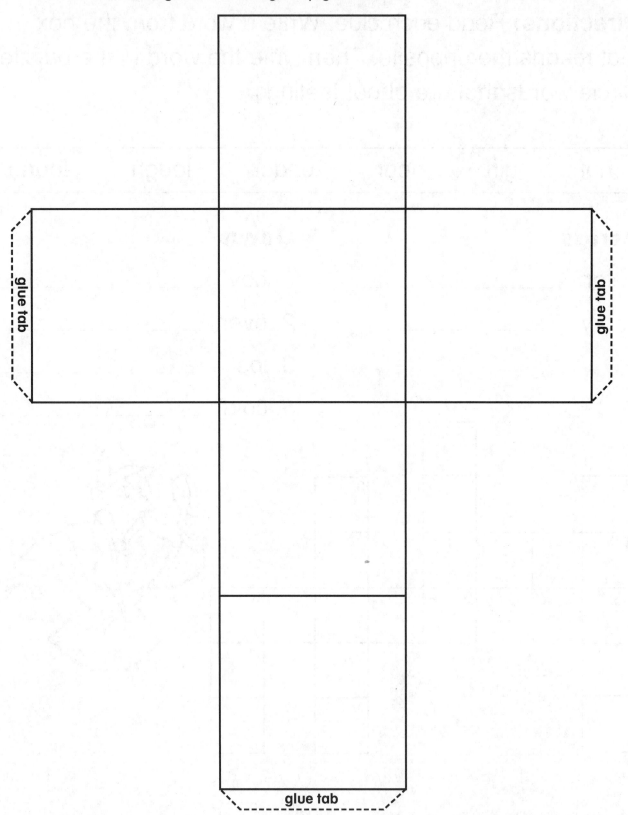

glue tab

glue tab

glue tab

Unit 3, Face the Feelings: Pattern
Three Cheers for August 1–2, SV 9835-3

Family Facts

 A family is a group of people who love and care for one another and depend on each other. The main job of the family is to take care of the basic needs of love, food, shelter, clothing, companionship, and protection.

 A family can be made up of different numbers of people. A family can have as few as two people.

 Some children live with other relatives, like grandparents, cousins, or aunts and uncles. Other children may live with friends.

 The largest known family is recorded in the *Guinness Book of World Records*. One woman had thirty-two children.

 American families have an average of two children.

 A nuclear family consists of two generations, usually a mother, a father, and children.

 A family made up of stepparents and/or stepchildren is called a blended family.

 Grandparents, aunts, uncles, and cousins make up an extended family.

 The First Family is the family of the President of the United States.

 Geographic features, climatic conditions, and natural resources influence how a family lives.

 A family tree is a diagram that shows how all the members and ancestors of a family are related.

 Families around the world have different ideals and traditions. They celebrate different holidays, or they may celebrate the same holidays in different ways. These differences may come from their ethnic backgrounds or religious beliefs.

People in My Family

Materials

- pattern on page 50
- brown and white construction paper
- crayons
- scissors
- glue

Directions

Teacher Preparation: Duplicate a brown and a white house pattern for each child.

1. Cut two large doors in the brown house. Open the flaps and make a crease to keep the doors open.

2. Lay the brown house on the white house so the edges are even. Trace the opening.

3. Remove the brown house. Draw a picture of all the people in your family inside the traced area of the white paper.

4. Make a glue line around the sides and top of the white house.

5. Lay the brown house on the white house again so the edges are even. Press the pieces together. Make sure that the door flaps do not get glue on them.

I Can Help

Materials

- patterns on page 51
- chart paper
- 2-gallon plastic jugs
- stickers
- construction paper
- art and craft supplies
- glue
- scissors
- markers

Directions

Teacher Preparation: Duplicate the hand patterns on a variety of colors of construction paper. Cut the hands apart and place them in a pile. Cut out a side of each milk jug to provide each child with a "jar" to decorate. Lead children in a discussion of the kinds of jobs they can do around the house to help their families. Record the responses on chart paper.

1. Select two or three paper hands. Cut them out.

2. Decorate the hands.

3. Glue the hands on a plastic jar.

4. Use other art supplies and stickers to decorate the jar.

Save children's job jars and the chart paper to use with "Jobs for Me" on page 48.

Family Tree Salad

You will need

- baby spinach leaves
- celery
- carrots
- salad dressings
- paper plates
- plastic forks
- knife

Directions

Teacher Preparation: Cut the celery into 6-inch stalks. Cut the carrots into circles.

1. Place a celery stalk on a paper plate for a tree trunk.

2. Arrange spinach leaves on the plate for the tree leaves.

3. Count out and take ten carrot circles.

4. Work with a partner. Say the name of a family member and place a carrot circle on the "tree" for the person.

5. Pour some salad dressing on the plate. Enjoy!

Note: Be aware of children who may have food allergies.

Three Cheers for August 1–2, SV 9835-3

Family Chant

A family works.

A family plays.

A family shows love

   in so many ways!

A family helps.

A family shares.

Because everyone in

   a family cares!

Note: Once children learn the words, challenge them to do the chant as a round. Divide the class in half and have the second group begin the chant after the first group finishes the first verse.

Fun Families to Read About

Arthur's Family Vacation
by Marc Brown (Little, Brown)

A Chair for My Mother
by Vera Williams (HarperTrophy)

The Kissing Hand
by Audrey Penn (Child and Family Press)

Meet the Barkers
by Tomie dePaola (Penguin Putnam)

In My Family
by Carmen Lomas Garza (Children's Book Press)

Song and Dance Man
by Karen Ackerman (Alfred A. Knopf)

Mufaro's Beautiful Daughters: An African Tale
by John Steptoe (Scholastic)

Nana Upstairs & Nana Downstairs
by Tomie dePaola (Putnam)

The New Baby
by Mercer Meyer (Golden Books)

Over the Moon
by Karen Katz (Henry Holt & Company)

The Relatives Came
by Cynthia Rylant (Pearson Learning)

44

A Family . . .

Materials

- pattern on page 50
- craft paper
- black construction paper
- markers and crayons

- 2 complimentary colors of crepe streamers
- drawing paper

- scissors
- stapler
- border

Directions

Teacher Preparation: Cover the bulletin board in craft paper. Add a border and the caption. Trace the house pattern in the center of the board. Draw paper doll figures to show one adult and two children on black paper and cut them out. Overlay the streamers and twist them to make the board divisions and the border. Staple them in place. Add the captions "plays!", "works!", "helps!", and "shares!" Review the chant on page 44 with children.

1. Draw a picture of a favorite way that your family spends time together.

2. Write or dictate a sentence that tells about your picture.

Allow children time to share their pictures with the class and identify in which section of the board the picture belongs. Help them staple their pictures to the corresponding section.

Family Centers

Language Center

Language Arts Standard
Recognizes rhyming words

Rhyme Time Families

Materials

• activity master on page 52

Teacher Preparation: Duplicate the activity master for each child.

Review the picture names. Invite children to change the first letter in each group to make a list of rhyming words that name the pictures.

Math Center

Math Standard
Understands the relationship of parts to the whole

Family Shares

Materials

• activity master on page 53
• counters
• crayons or markers

Teacher Preparation: Duplicate the activity master for each child.

Tell children to divide the pizza into equal parts so each family member gets the same amount. To help children you may want to have them put a counter on each family member, and then move the counters to equal spacing on the pizzas.

Family Centers

Science Center

Science Standard
Sorts organisms according to their parts and characteristics

Animal Families

Materials

- picture cards on page 54
- markers or crayons
- construction paper
- scissors

Teacher Preparation: Duplicate on construction paper, color, and cut apart the animal picture cards.

Invite children to match the animal families.

Social Studies Center

Social Studies Standard
Describes how household tools and appliances have changed the way families live

Family Jobs Long Ago

Materials

- activity master on page 55
- scissors
- glue

Teacher Preparation: Duplicate the activity master for each child.

Lead children in a discussion of the pictures showing household tools of the past. Then have children cut apart the pictures of the tools that help families do the jobs today and glue them next to the pictures of the past.

Family Centers

Writing Center

Language Arts Standard
Identifies and writes simple sentences

Jobs for Me

Materials

- job chart and job jar completed in "I Can Help" on page 42
- patterns on page 51
- construction paper
- scissors

Teacher Preparation: Duplicate a page of hands for each child on construction paper.

Review the ways that people in the family help each other. Read the list of responses written on the chart. Then have children cut out the hands and write a job they can do to help at home on each hand. Have them place the hands inside their job jars. Suggest that they take their job jars home and do one job each day.

Technology Center

Technology Standard
Uses a variety of input devices such as mouse, keyboard, and disk drive

Family Names

Materials

- computer
- chart paper
- marker

Teacher Preparation: Write descriptive family names on chart paper, such as *father, mother, sister, brother, grandfather*, and *grandmother*. Include other descriptive names of people who may be part of children's families.

Point out the names on the chart and discuss the relationships. Invite children to type a list of descriptive names of family members who live with them. Challenge them to type the familiar names beside the descriptive names.

Family Centers

Art Center

Art Standard
Increases manipulative skill, using a variety of materials to produce drawings, paintings, prints, and constructives

Picture Frame

Materials

- craft sticks
- sequins
- wood glue
- paper (optional)

- markers
- glitter
- glue
- crayons (optional)

Have children form a square frame with four craft sticks and glue them together at the corners. Tell them to set aside the frames to dry. Later, invite children to color the front of the frame with markers and glue on glitter and sequins. Children may wish to color a picture to place inside the frame.

Communication Center

Social Studies Standard
Expresses ideas orally based on knowledge and experiences

Famous Families

Materials

- books with familiar stories involving families, including *Little Red Riding Hood*, *The Three Bears*, *The Three Billy Goats Gruff*, and *Jack and the Beanstalk*

Teacher Preparation: Place the books on a designated shelf or in a basket.

Invite partners to read or review the books and discuss how the people in the families help each other.

House Pattern

Use with "People in My Family" on page 42, "A Family" on page 45, "Houses in Mr. Plumbean's Neighborhood" on page 60, and "My Favorite Room" on page 63.

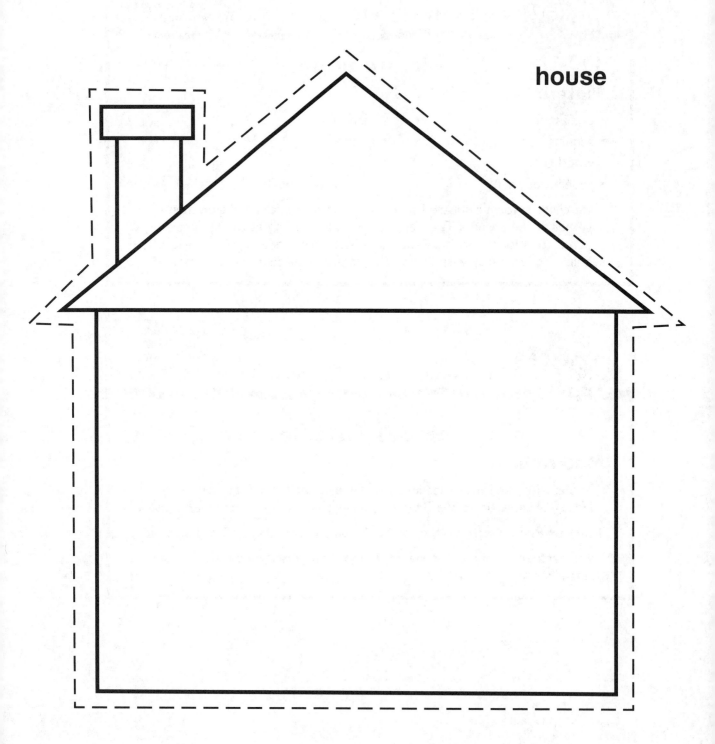

house

Hand Patterns

Use with "I Can Help" on page 42 and "Jobs for Me" on page 48.

hands

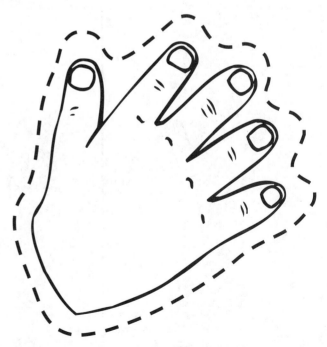

Name _____ Date _____

Fun Word Families

Directions: Say each picture name. Change the first letter of each word. Write the picture name.

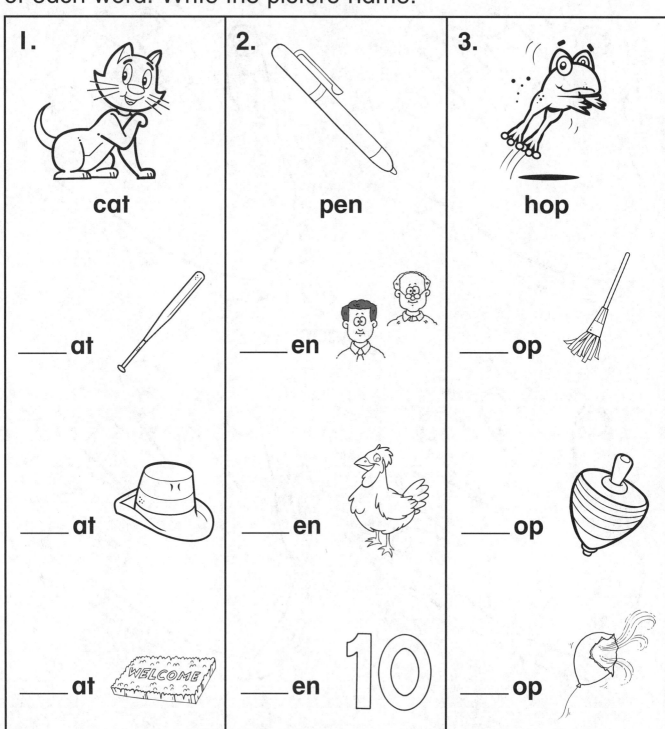

1. cat

___at

___at

___at

2. pen

___en

___en

___en

3. hop

___op

___op

___op

Use with "Rhyme Time Families" on page 46.

Unit 4, In a Family: Activity Master
Three Cheers for August 1–2, SV 9835-3

Name _____ **Date** _____

Pizza Parts

Directions: How many people are in each family? Cut the pizza so that everyone gets an equal part.

1.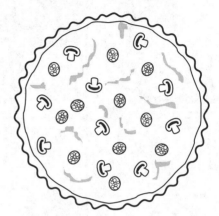

2.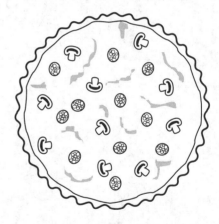

3.

Use with "Family Shares" on page 46.

Animal Picture Cards

Use with "Animal Families" on page 47.

Unit 4, In a Family: Cards
Three Cheers for August 1–2, SV 9835-3

Jobs Then and Now

Directions: Look at the pictures that show how jobs were done long ago. Cut apart the pictures at the bottom of the page. Glue the pictures to show the tool we use today to do the same job.

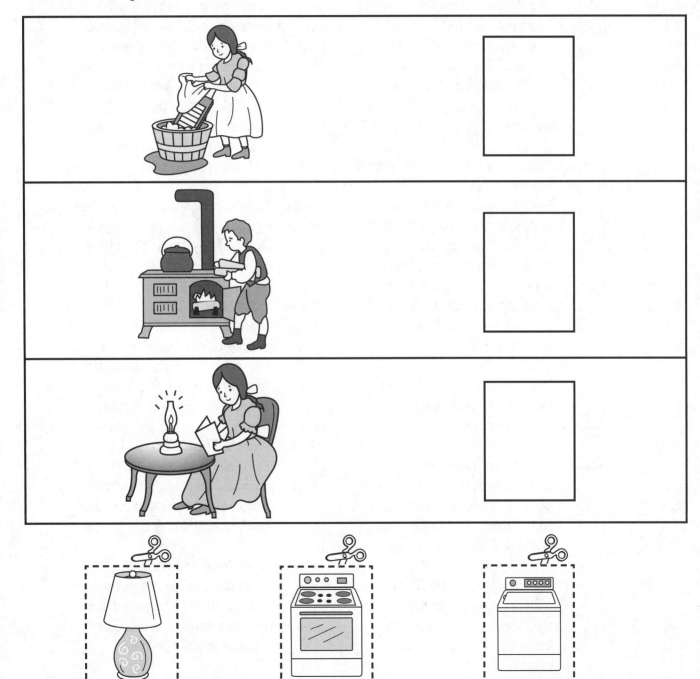

Use with "Family Jobs Long Ago" on page 47.

Unit 4, In a Family: Activity Master

Three Cheers for August 1–2, SV 9835-3

Facts That Will Floor You

 People who live in the desert use sand and mud mixed with water to build their houses. They either make bricks that they stack, or they spread the wet mixture over a frame.

 People who live on the plains use tall, thick grass to build their houses. They bundle stems of grass together into sheaths. They lay the sheaths on a wooden frame. Then they cover the grass with mud. Many of these places do not get much rain, so houses last a long time.

 In Korea, some houses are heated by building a fire on a stone floor.

 In Malaysia, houses near the water are built on stilts, or poles. If the water rises due to a storm, the water does not enter the house.

 Some people in the Bagobo tribe in the Philippines, live in treehouses. They stay safe from animals, insects, and other tribes that may try to harm them.

 Some people move a lot because they follow herds of animals. When the animals move, the people must follow. Their houses have to move, too. They often build their houses with a timber frame and cover it with animal skins to form a large tent.

 The Native Americans in the Arctic build homes with ice blocks. They stack the blocks to make igloos.

 Most people think that only bears live in caves. Some people have turned a cave into a house that has all the appliances and living features of a contemporary house.

 The traditional house in Mongolia is round. It has a chimney through the center. People in Mongolia paint the front door red.

 The White House is the most famous house in the United States. That is where the President of the United States and his family live.

All Around the House

Materials

- clean, small milk cartons
- white construction paper
- scrap paper
- markers or crayons
- scissors
- glue

Directions

Teacher Preparation: Cover each milk carton in white construction paper.

1. Draw bricks, rocks, shingles, wood planks, or other coverings to match how your house looks on the outside.

2. Cut out windows and doors. Glue them on your house.

Model House Mural

Materials

- craft paper
- recycled magazines and catalogs
- index cards
- marker
- scissors
- glue

Directions

Teacher Preparation: Draw a two-story house outline on paper and include a kitchen, living room, dining room, bathroom, laundry room, and three bedrooms. Label each room. Cut index cards into fourths.

Display the house. Point out to children the name of each room. Lead them in a discussion of the kinds of appliances and furniture that might be found in each room.

1. Look in magazines and catalogs for pictures of items that you would find in the different rooms of a house.

2. Cut out three pictures.

3. Glue the pictures in the correct rooms.

Note: Discuss the completed pictures and write labels for them on index cards. Attach the labels. Then invite children to cut out and glue additional pictures of furniture, appliances, and decorative elements in the appropriate rooms.

Apartment Living

You will need

- wheat sandwich bread
- pimento cheese spread
- square-shaped cheese crackers
- rectangle-shaped crackers
- paper plates
- craft sticks

Directions

Teacher Preparation: Break the rectangle-shaped crackers into separate rectangles.

1. Place a slice of bread on a plate.

2. Spread the pimento cheese on the bread.

3. Place a rectangle-shaped cracker on the bread to make a door.

4. Place cheese crackers on the bread for windows.

Note: Be aware of children who may have food allergies.

Who "Woodn't" Want to Read These Books?

A House Is a House for Me
by Mary Ann Hoberman (Penguin)

Annabel Again
by Janice Boland (Dial)

Castles, Caves, and Honeycombs
by Linda Ashman (Harcourt)

Homes Around the World
by Bobbie Kalman (Crabtree Publishing)

Raise the Roof
by Anastasia Suen (Viking)

This Is My House
by Arthur Dorros (Scholastic)

We Were Tired of Living in a House
by Liesel Moak Skorpen (Putnam)

58

This Is the House That Jack (and His Friends) Built

This is the house that Jack built.

This is the architect, who used a pencil to draw the plans,
    just for the house that Jack built.

This is the carpenter, who used a saw to cut the wood,
    after the architect, who used a pencil to draw the plans,
        just for the house that Jack built.

This is the roofer, who used a hammer to pound the shingles,
    after the carpenter, who used a saw to cut the wood,
        after the architect, who used a pencil to draw the plans,
            just for the house that Jack built.

This is the plumber, who used a wrench to put in the sinks,
    after the roofer, who used a hammer to pound the shingles,
        after the carpenter, who used a saw to cut the wood,
            after the architect, who used a pencil to draw the plans,
                just for the house that Jack built.

This is the electrician, who used a screwdriver to hang the lights,
    after the plumber, who used a wrench to put in the sinks,
        after the roofer, who used a hammer to pound the shingles,
            after the carpenter, who used a saw to cut the wood,
                after the architect, who used a pencil to draw the plans,
                    just for the house that Jack built.

This is the painter, who used a brush to paint the house,
    after the electrician, who used a screwdriver to hang the lights,
        after the plumber, who used a wrench to put in the sinks,
            after the roofer, who used a hammer to pound the shingles,
                after the carpenter, who used a saw to cut the wood,
                  after the architect, who used a pencil to draw the plans,
                    just for the house that Jack built.

Note: Use the patterns on page 65 to make puppets that children can color and hold or see during the poem.

Houses in Mr. Plumbean's Neighborhood

Materials

- *The Big Orange Splot* by Daniel Pinkwater (Scholastic)
- pattern on page 50
- white construction paper
- white craft paper
- black tempera paint
- border
- art supplies (glitter, ribbon, buttons, etc.)
- markers and crayons
- paintbrushes
- scissors
- glue
- stapler

Directions

Teacher Preparation: Duplicate a house pattern on white construction paper for each child. Cover the bulletin board in craft paper. Add a border. Paint a black road network. Add the caption along with the book title and author's name in the corner. Read aloud *The Big Orange Splot* to children.

1. Think about the way you would decorate your house if you lived in Plumbean's neighborhood.

2. Cut out a house.

3. Draw windows and doors.

4. Use the art supplies to make your house special.

Allow children time to share their houses with the class. Help them staple their pictures along the roads on the bulletin board.

House Centers

Language Center

Language Arts Standard
Knows the order of the alphabet

Alphabet House

Materials

- activity master on page 66
- crayons

Teacher Preparation: Duplicate the activity master for each child.

Have children connect the dots from *a* to *z* to complete the picture. Then invite them to color it.

Math Center

Math Standard
Identifies basic geometric shapes

Shapes We See

Materials

- activity master on page 67
- crayons

Teacher Preparation: Duplicate the activity master for each child.

Have children count each shape and write the number that tells how many. Then invite them to color the picture.

House Centers

Science Center

Science Standard
Identifies characteristics of
living organisms

Animal Homes

Materials

- picture cards on page 68
- markers
- construction paper
- scissors

Teacher Preparation: Duplicate on construction paper, color, and cut apart the animal and home picture cards.

Invite children to match the animal to the home in which it lives.

Social Studies Center

Social Studies Standard
Identifies examples of and
uses for natural resources

Houses Around the World

Materials

- activity master on page 69
- scissors
- glue

Teacher Preparation: Duplicate the activity master for each child.

Lead children in a discussion of the kind of climate and landforms they see in the pictures. Then have them cut apart the pictures of the houses and glue them in the scenes in which they belong.

House Centers

Writing Center

Language Arts Standard
Identifies and writes simple sentences

My Favorite Room

Materials

- pattern on page 50
- crayons
- white construction paper

Teacher Preparation: Duplicate the house pattern on construction paper for each child.

Invite children to draw a picture of their favorite room in the house. Then ask them to dictate or write a sentence telling why it is special.

Technology Center

Technology Standard
Uses a variety of input devices such as mouse, keyboard, and disk drive

I Live Here

Materials

- pattern on page 25
- computer, mouse, and keyboard
- children's addresses

Teacher Preparation: Duplicate the computer pattern for each child. For children unfamiliar with their address, write it on the monitor of the computer pattern.

Discuss with children why houses, apartment buildings, offices, and stores have addresses. Then, ask them why they should know their address for safety purposes. Next, have them write their address on the monitor of the computer pattern. Invite children to type their address at least three times into the computer using different font sizes.

House Centers

Literacy Center

Social Studies Standard
Expresses ideas orally based on knowledge and experiences

Piggy House Troubles

Materials

- *The Three Little Pigs* books
- crayons
- drawing paper

Ask children to review *The Three Little Pigs*. Tell them to draw an example of each kind of house. Then have them discuss why two of the houses did not stand up against the wolf's blowing, while one house did. Then have them brainstorm a list of things that would be important to have in a sturdy, safe house.

Game Center

Math Standard
Combines geometric shapes to make new geometric shapes using concrete models

A Shapely House

Materials

- pattern on page 70
- large paper clip
- pencil
- small shape blocks that match shapes on the pattern

Teacher Preparation: Duplicate the pattern several times.

Demonstrate for children how to make a spinner by placing a large paper clip on the circle and holding the point of a pencil inside the clip on the dot. Then point out the shapes used to build the house on the game board. Tell children they get a shape when the spinner lands on it. The first player to build the house as shown wins.

House Builders Patterns

Use with "The House That Jack (and His Friends) Built" on page 59.

architect

roofer

carpenter

plumber

electrician

Jack and his house

Unit 5, House, Sweet House: Patterns
Three Cheers for August 1–2, SV 9835-3

Name _____ Date _____

Dot-to-Dot Fun

Directions: Draw lines to join the dots from **a** to **z** to complete the picture. Then color the picture.

Use with "Alphabet House" on page 61.

Unit 5, House, Sweet House: Activity Master
Three Cheers for August 1–2, SV 9835-3

Name _____ **Date** _____

House Shapes

Directions: Count each shape. Write the number. Then color the picture.

Use with "Shapes We See" on page 61.

Unit 5, House, Sweet House: Activity Master
Three Cheers for August 1–2, SV 9835-3

Animals and Their Homes Picture Cards

Use with "Animal Homes" on page 62.

bear

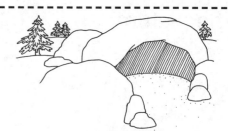

cave

bird

nest

rabbit

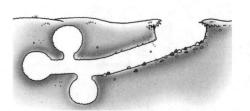

burrow

fish

seaweed

beaver

dam

Unit 5, House, Sweet House: Cards
Three Cheers for August 1–2, SV 9835-3

What Kind of House?

Directions: Cut apart the pictures of the houses and glue them in the scenes in which they belong.

Use with "Houses Around the World" on page 62.

Build a House Game Pattern

Use with "A Shapely House" on page 64.

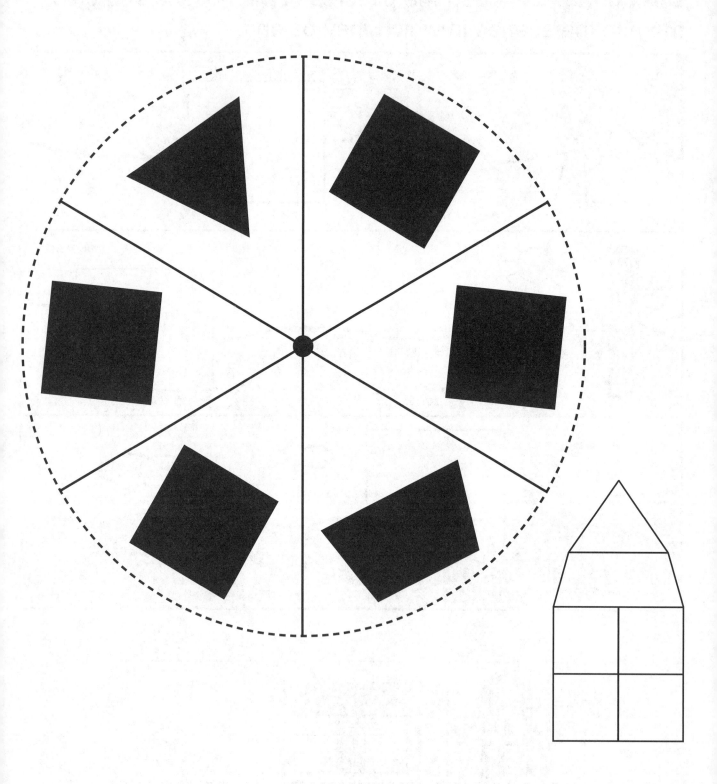

Unit 5, House, Sweet House: Pattern
Three Cheers for August 1–2, SV 9835-3

Pet Facts

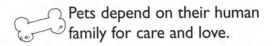

- Pets depend on their human family for care and love.

- A pet is a living creature, not a toy.

- A doctor who takes care of pets is called a veterinarian.

- The first cats became pets 3,000 to 4,000 years ago in ancient Egypt.

- Dogs are probably the descendants of gray wolves.

- The relationship between humans and dogs goes back nearly 10,000 years. Scientists have concluded this because cave paintings clearly show dogs hunting with humans.

- People have pets for many reasons, including companionship, social interaction, and safety.

- Today there are many kinds of pets. Some of the more interesting pets include potbellied pigs, iguanas, lizards, and snakes.

- Some dogs are pets as well as workers. Many dogs are trained to help people who cannot see, hear, or move lead more fulfilling and independent lives.

- Puppies who will become companions for persons who have a disability are cared for by puppy raisers. Puppy raisers are volunteer families that provide puppies with basic necessities for the first year. They must love the puppies and teach them basic manners. The puppy raisers also must take the puppies to all kinds of places where they are exposed to noise and lots of people.

- In the United States, the Labrador retriever is the most popular breed of dog.

The Bremen Town Musician Puppets

Materials

- patterns on page 80
- white construction paper
- crayons or markers
- craft sticks
- glue
- scissors

Directions

Teacher Preparation: Duplicate the patterns on construction paper for each child.

1. Color and cut out each puppet.

2. Glue a craft stick to the back of each puppet. Set the puppets aside to dry.

Note: Children will use the puppets in "Retell a Story" on page 77 to retell the story of the "Bremen Town Musicians."

Pet Needs Mobile

Materials

- patterns on pages 81 and 82
- hangers
- white construction paper
- scrap construction paper
- crayons or markers
- yarn
- tape
- scissors

Directions

Teacher Preparation: Duplicate multiple copies of the pet patterns on white construction paper. Cut them apart. Lead children in a discussion of things that pets need. Include the intrinsic needs of love and exercise as well as the specific needs for everyday care, such as food and water. Provide a hanger for each child.

1. Choose a pet picture or draw one of your own.

2. Color and cut out a picture of the pet. Tape it to the hook of the hanger.

3. Draw and cut out all of the things that the pet needs.

4. Cut a piece of yarn for each picture.

5. Tape a piece of yarn to the back of each picture.

6. Tie the yarn to the hanger.

Three Cheers for August 1–2, SV 9835-3

Kitty Cat Salad

You will need

- canned pear halves
- raisins
- celery
- knife
- cutting board
- paper plates

Directions

Teacher Preparation: Cut some pears into quarters to make the cat's ears. Slice celery to make the cat's eyes. Provide a paper plate for each child.

1. Place a pear half on a plate with the round side faceup.

2. Get two pear quarters. Place them with the round edges against the top of the pear half to make the ears.

3. Get two pieces of celery. Place them on the pear half to make the eyes.

4. Use raisins to make the nose and mouth.

Note: Be aware of children who may have food allergies.

Three Cheers for August 1–2, SV 9835-3

Pet Riddles

I bought a pet that splishes and splashes.

It likes to swim around.

Can you guess which pet I bought?

It doesn't make a sound.

I bought a pet that jumps and plays.

It barks and chases sticks.

Can you guess which pet I bought?

My pet kisses when it licks.

I bought a pet that chirps and flies.

A cage is where it stays.

Can you guess which pet I bought?

I feed it seeds each day.

I bought a pet that plays with string.

It likes to sleep and purr.

Can you guess which pet I bought?

It has the softest fur.

I have a pet that squeaks and hides.

It runs in a plastic trail.

Can you guess which pet I bought?

It has a long, long tail.

Note: Duplicate copies of the pet patterns on pages 81 and 82 for each child. Ask children to color and cut out the pets. Invite them to hold up the correct pet picture to answer each riddle.

Purr-fectly Good Pet Books

Arthur's Pet Business
by Marc Brown (Little, Brown & Co.)

The Best Pet of All
by David LaRochelle (Dutton)

Harry the Dirty Dog
by Gene Zion (HarperCollins)

Henry and Mudge
by Cynthia Rylant (Aladdin)

Perfect Pets
by Nancy Elizabeth Wallace
(Winslow Press)

Pet Show
by Ezra Jack Keats (Puffin)

The Pet Vet
by Marcia Leonard (Millbrook Press)

Whistle for Willie
by Ezra Jack Keats (Viking)

Who Wants Arthur?
by Amanda Graham (Gareth Stevens)

Pets We Have

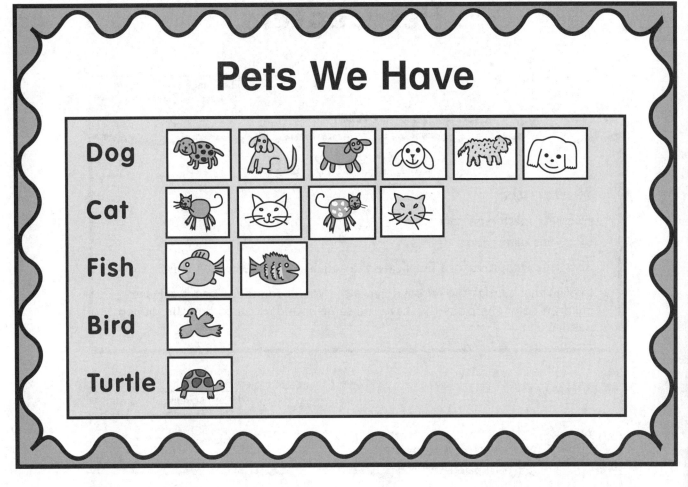

Materials

- white construction paper
- crayons or markers
- border
- stapler
- scissors
- craft paper

Directions

Teacher Preparation: Cover the board with the craft paper. Add a decorative border. Draw the frame for a picture graph. Write the animal names for the categories and a graph title. Cut each sheet of construction paper in half. Instruct children to draw the picture horizontally. For children who do not have pets, suggest they draw a picture of the pet they would like to have.

1. Get a half of a sheet of paper for each pet you have.

2. Draw a picture of each pet on separate sheets of paper. Be sure that the paper lies horizontally.

3. Find the animal name on the graph and staple the picture(s) on the graph.

Note: Once the graph is complete, ask children questions about the data.

Pet Centers

Language Center

Language Arts Standard
Recognizes short vowel sounds

Cat Sound Off

Materials

- activity master on page 83
- crayons or markers

Teacher Preparation: Duplicate the activity master for each child.

Explain that *cat* has the /a/ sound. It is the vowel sound for short *a*. Have children color the parts that have the same sound as *cat* to find the hidden picture.

Math Center

Math Standard
Understands how to measure using nonstandard and standard units

Mice Measure

Materials

- mouse pattern on page 81
- yarn
- 1-inch connecting cubes or ruler
- glue
- gray paper
- file folder
- scissors

Teacher Preparation: Trace and cut out six mice (without the tails) from the gray paper. Cut six pieces of yarn into 8-inch lengths. Glue a piece of yarn to each mouse to make a tail. Glue the mice in a row on the inside of a folder along the top edge. Number them in order from 1 to 6. Decide if the children will measure with cubes or a ruler. If using cubes to measure, join the cubes to make six different lengths. Cut off each "tail" to match one of the cube trains or inch measurements. Vary the tail lengths so they are in random order.

Have children number a piece of paper from 1 to 6. Tell them to measure each tail and record the number.

Pet Centers

Science Center

Science Standard
Understands organisms and their environments

A Fishy Home

Materials

- patterns on page 84
- crayons or markers
- scissors
- stapler
- tape
- large paper plates
- blue plastic wrap or cellophane
- glue

Teacher Preparation: Duplicate the aquarium pieces for each child.

Have children cut off the top quarter of a paper plate to make a fishbowl. Explain that the cut piece will be the fishbowl base, but to set it aside temporarily. Then, tell them to color and cut out the plants, rocks, and fish. Invite them to glue the cutouts in the fishbowl to make a home for the fish. Next, have them tape a piece of blue plastic wrap on the fishbowl for water. Finally, have them staple the paper-plate base to the fishbowl.

Social Studies Center

Social Studies Standard
Reads and listens to literature, including multicultural works, folk tales, and ballads

Retell a Story

Materials

- puppets (completed in "The Bremen Town Musician Puppets" on page 72)
- picture book copies of *The Bremen Town Musicians*
- puppet stage or a sheet and two chairs

Teacher Preparation: If a puppet stage is unavailable, create one by spreading a sheet over two chairs.

Invite children to review the different books and discuss how they are alike and different. Then invite children to take turns presenting their own versions of *The Bremen Town Musicians*.

Pet Centers

Writing Center

Language Arts Standard
Uses capitalization and punctuation correctly

More Pet Riddles

Materials

Review the different riddles on page 74. Challenge children to write riddles of their own. Point out that their riddles do not have to rhyme.

Technology Standard
Uses tools such as real objects, manipulatives, and technology to solve problems

Technology Center

Pet Care Costs

Materials

- activity master on page 85
- calculator
- pet supply catalogs and ads
- glue
- mobiles (completed in "Pet Needs Mobile" on page 72)
- scissors

Teacher Preparation: Duplicate the activity master for each child.

Have children draw a picture of the animal shown on their mobiles in the center of the web. Then, tell children to look at the items on their mobiles. Ask them to find an example of four of those items in the catalogs or ads and cut the pictures out. Have them glue the pictures on the web and write the prices. Next, challenge children to use the calculator to add the prices of the items. Have them write the total in the center of the web.

Pet Centers

Art Center

Art Standard
Uses a variety of mediums to create art

Feather Painting

Materials

- feathers
- tempera paint
- drawing paper

Invite children to paint a picture of a bird using feathers.

Physical Development Skills Center

Math Standard
Counts by 2s, 5s, and 10s

Skip Count Rabbit

Materials

- rabbit pattern on page 81
- white construction paper
- tape
- scissors

Teacher Preparation: Enlarge the rabbit pattern so that it is the size of a sheet of construction paper. Make 20 copies of the rabbit and cut them out. Choose a skip count sequence and write the numbers on the rabbits. Tape the rabbits on the floor in random order, making sure that children can easily jump to them in skip count order.

Have children take turns jumping to the rabbits in skip count order. They can jump forwards or backwards. Challenge them to say the number names before jumping.

Puppet Patterns

Use with "The Bremen Town Musician Puppets" on page 72.

dog

cat

robbers

rooster

donkey

Unit 6, Perfect Pets: Patterns
Three Cheers for August 1–2, SV 9835-3

Pet Patterns

Use with "Pet Needs Mobile" on page 72, "Pet Riddles" on page 74, "Mice Measure" on page 76, and "Skip Count Rabbit" on page 79.

mouse

cat

rabbit

dog

fish

81

Pet Patterns

Use with "Pet Needs Mobile" on page 72 and "Pet Riddles" on page 74.

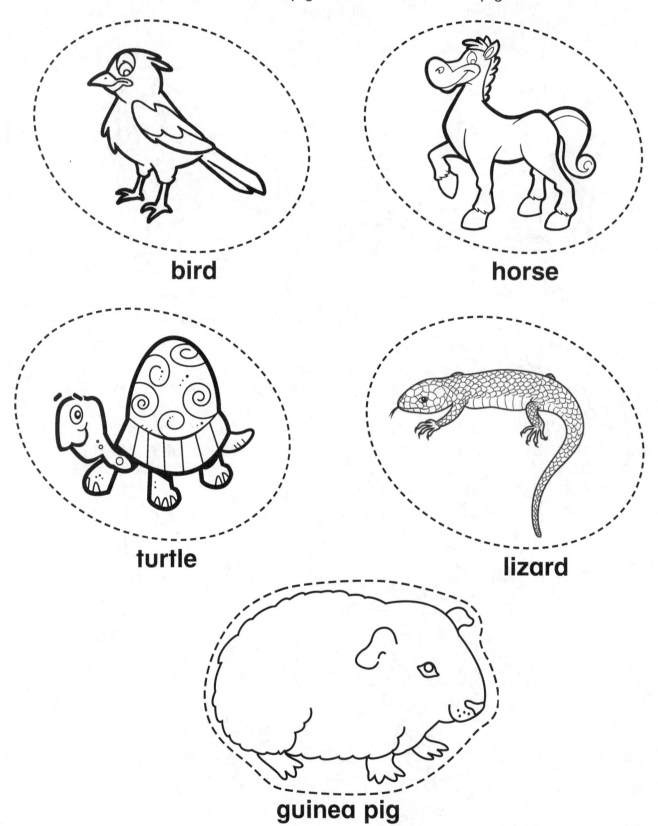

bird

horse

turtle

lizard

guinea pig

Unit 6, Perfect Pets: Patterns
Three Cheers for August 1–2, SV 9835-3

Name _____ Date _____

Cat Sounds

Directions: What is hiding? Color the parts in which the word has the short **a** sound as in **cat.**

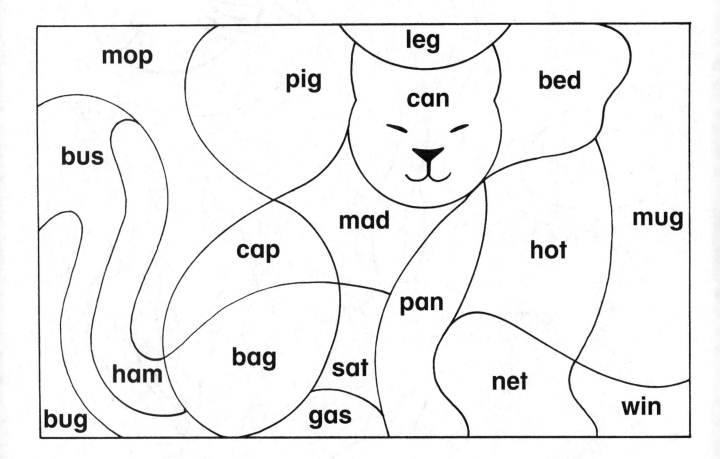

Use with "Cat Sound Off" on page 76.

Unit 6, Perfect Pets: Activity Master
Three Cheers for August 1–2, SV 9835-3

Aquarium Patterns

Use with "A Fishy Home" on page 77.

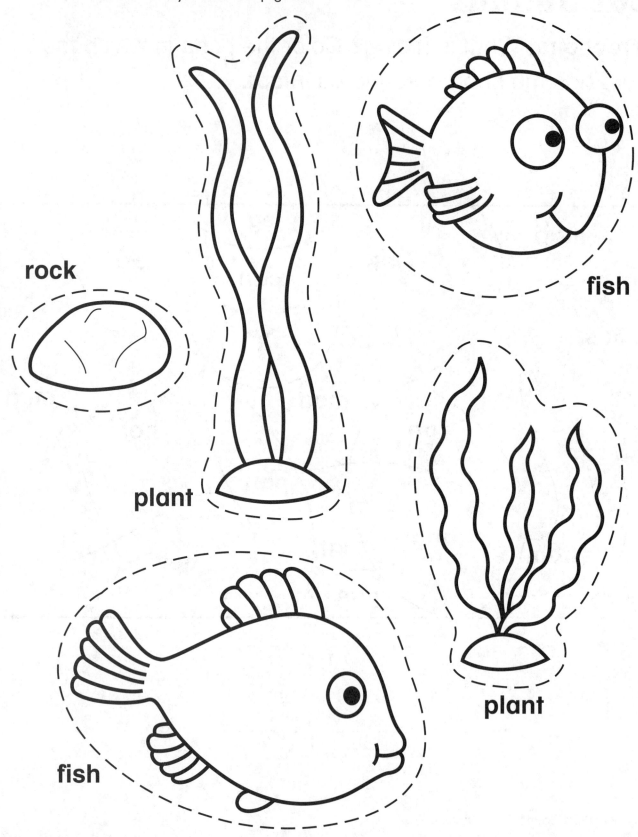

rock

plant

fish

fish

plant

Name _____ **Date** _____

Pet Costs

Directions: Draw your pet in the center of the web. Cut out 4 pictures of things your pet needs. Glue the pictures in the web. Write the prices. Add the prices with a calculator. Write the total.

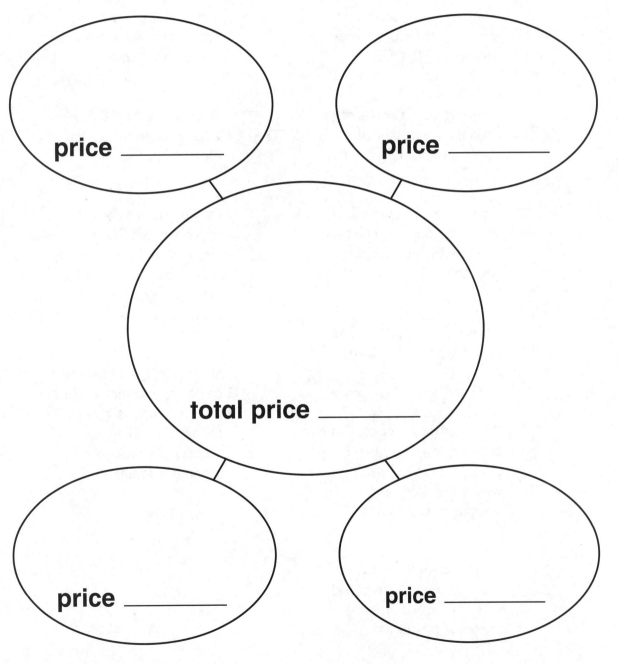

price _____

price _____

total price _____

price _____

price _____

Use with "Pet Care Costs" on page 78.

A Look at Donald Crews

 Donald Crews, a well-known African-American children's author and illustrator, was born in Newark, New Jersey, on August 30, 1938.

 Growing up, Crews always used his hands to make things and draw.

 Crews's father worked for a train company, so Crews had lots of experiences with trains.

 Crews is married and has two daughters, Nina and Amy.

 When writing a book, Crews explores ways to visually develop a topic. Then he writes the story and completes the pictures.

 He is known for his vibrant use of primary colors and shapes to make visually appealing posterlike graphics.

 Crews generally focuses on machines of the twentieth century, but two of his books, *Bigmama's* and *Shortcut*, are autobiographical.

 Truck and *School Bus* have been chosen as Caldecott Honor Books.

 Freight Train was also an Honor Book. *Freight Train* was inspired by Crews's many childhood train trips from New Jersey to Florida to visit his grandmother.

 His books are popular for beginning readers as they have few words, giving children a feeling of successful reading accomplishment.

Literature Selection: *Bigmama's* by Donald Crews

Explain that *Bigmama's* is a book that tells about Donald Crews when he was a boy. Then read the book out loud. Point out the activities that the family members do together. Also discuss the emotions that the different characters feel and how the author communicates the feelings. Then have children do the following activities.

Train Time Travel

Materials

- pattern on page 90
- United States map
- pushpins
- yarn
- chart paper
- markers
- crayons
- scissors

Directions

Teacher Preparation: Duplicate the activity master for each child.

Remind children that it took Crews and his family three days and two nights to travel by train from his home in Newark, New Jersey, to reach Cottondale, Florida. Then find the two locations on a map and mark the places with pushpins. Measure the distance with a length of yarn. Invite children to brainstorm a list of activities that Crews and his family might have done during the train trip. Record the responses on a chart. Next, find the town where your school is located and mark it with a third pushpin. Compare the distances between Newark and Cottondale and between your town and Cottondale using the yarn measure. Discuss with children how long the trip from your town to Cottondale might take on the same train as in the story.

1. Think about something that you would do with your family on a train trip.

2. Draw a picture of it. Color the picture.

3. Write or dictate a sentence about your picture.

Grandparent Stories

Materials

- activity master on page 91
- crayons

Directions

Teacher Preparation: Duplicate the activity master for each child.

Remind children that *Bigmama's* is a story that Donald Crews wrote about himself and his experiences when visiting his grandparents. Review some of the activities shared in the story.

1. Think about something special that you have done with a grandparent or an older adult.

2. Draw a picture of it. Color the picture.

3. Write or dictate a sentence about your picture.

Books by Donald Crews

- *Bicycle Race* (William Morrow)

- *Bigmama's* (HarperTrophy)
  (This book can be used with the In a Family unit. See page 87 for additional ideas.)

- *Carousel* (Greenwillow)

- *Flying* (HarperTrophy)

- *Freight Train* (Greenwillow) Caldecott Honor Book

- *Harbor* (HarperTrophy)

- *Night Fair* (Greenwillow)

- *Parade* (HarperTrophy)

- *Sail Away* (HarperCollins)

- *School Bus* (HarperTrophy) Caldecott Honor Book
  (This book can be used with the Time for School unit.)

- *Shortcut* (HarperTrophy)
  (This book can be used with the In a Family or Face the Feelings units.)

- *Ten Black Dots* (HarperTrophy)
  (This book can be used with the Time for School unit as a math introduction.)

- *Truck* (Greenwillow) Caldecott Honor Book

- *We Read: A to Z* (Greenwillow)
  (This book can be used with the Time for School unit as a language arts introduction.)

Bookmark Patterns

"Crews-ing" through a good book by Donald Crews!

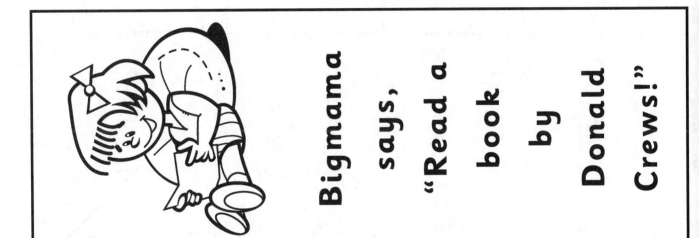

Bigmama says, "Read a book by Donald Crews!"

Flying high with books by Donald Crews!

Unit 7, Author Study: Patterns
Three Cheers for August 1–2, SV 9835-3

On a Train

Directions: Draw and color a picture of something you would do with your family on a train trip. Write or dictate a sentence about your picture.

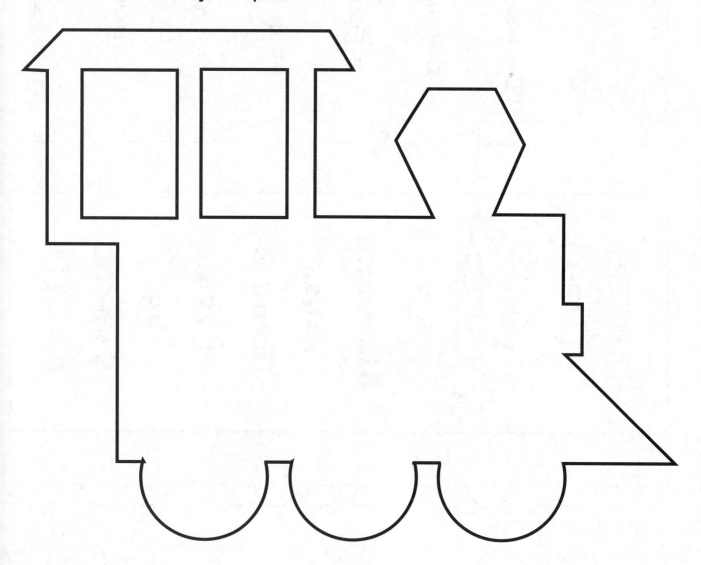

On a long train trip, I would

_____

_____.

Use with "Train Time Travel" on page 87.

Name _____ **Date** _____

A Special Grandparent

Directions: Draw and color a picture about something special you have done with a grandparent or an older adult.

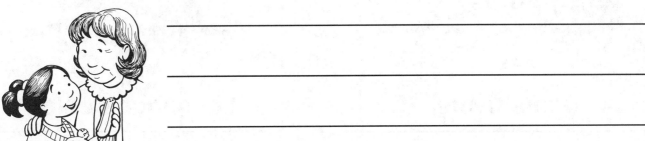

Use with "Grandparent Stories" on page 87.

Unit 7, Author Study: Activity Master
Three Cheers for August 1–2, SV 9835-3

Center Icons Patterns

Art Center

Communication Center

Game Center

Language Center

Center Icons Patterns

Literacy Center

Math Center

Music Center

Physical Development Skills Center

Center Icons Patterns

Science Center

Social Studies Center

Technology Center

Writing Center

Center Icons Patterns
Three Cheers for August 1–2, SV 9835-3

Student Awards

You're off to a good start in

_____.

_____
Teacher's signature

_____
Date

Congratulations, _____

Child's name

You are the August
Student of the Month for

_____.

_____
Teacher's signature

_____
Date

Student Award

Feel proud!
Feel happy!

_____
Child's name

can _____.

_____
Teacher's signature

_____
Date

Calendar Day Pattern

Suggested Uses
- Reproduce the card for each day of the month. Write the numerals on each card and place it on your class calendar. Use cards to mark special days.
- Reproduce to make cards to use in word ladders or word walls.
- Reproduce to make cards and write letters on each card. Children use the cards to play word games forming words.
- Reproduce to make cards to create matching or concentration games for children to use in activity centers. Choose from the following possible matching skills or create your own:
  — uppercase and lowercase letters
  — pictures of objects whose names rhyme, have the same beginning or ending sounds, or contain short or long vowels
  — pictures of adult animals and baby animals
  — number words and numerals
  — numerals and pictures of objects
  — colors and shapes
  — high-frequency sight words

Student Award/Calendar Day Patterns
Three Cheers for August 1–2, SV 9835-3